Walk Quietly the Beautiful Trail

Lyrics and Legends

Of the American Indian

Edited by C. Merton Babcock

With Authentic American Indian Art

Walk Quietly
The Beautiful Trail

♛ *Hallmark Editions*

WALK QUIETLY
THE BEAUTIFUL TRAIL

THE LIVING SPIRIT OF THE INDIAN
By Standing Bear,
Chief of the Oglala Sioux (1905-1939)

The feathered and blanketed figure of the American Indian has come to symbolize the American continent. He is the man who through centuries has been moulded and sculpted by the same hand that shaped the mountains, forests, and plains, and marked the course of its rivers.

The American Indian is of the soil, whether it be the region of forests, plains, pueblos, or mesas. He fits into the landscape, for the hand that fashioned the continent also fashioned the man for his surroundings. He once grew as naturally as the wild sunflowers; he belongs just as the buffalo belonged.

With a physique that fitted, the man developed fitting skills — crafts which today are called American. And the body had a soul, also formed and moulded by the same master hand of harmony. Out of the Indian approach to existence there came a great freedom — an intense and absorbing love for nature; a respect for life; enriching faith in a Supreme Power; and principles of truth, honesty, generosity, equity, and brotherhood. . . .

Becoming possessed of a fitting philosophy and art, it was by them that native man perpetuated his identity; stamped it into the history and soul of this country — made land and man one.

By living — struggling, losing, meditating, imbibing, aspiring, achieving — he wrote himself into the ineraseable evidence — an evidence that can be and often has been ignored, but never totally destroyed. . . .

The white man does not understand the Indian for the reason that he does not understand America. He is too far removed from its formative processes. The roots of the tree of his life have not yet grasped the rock and soil. The white man is still troubled with primitive fears; he still has in his consciousness the perils of this frontier continent, some of its fastnesses not yet having yielded to his questing footsteps and inquiring eyes. The man from Europe is still a foreigner and an alien.

But in the Indian the spirit of the land is still vested; it will be until other men are able to divine and meet its rhythms. . . .

When the Indian has forgotten the music of his forefathers, when the sound of the tom-tom is no more, when the memory of his heroes is no longer told in story . . . he will be dead. When from him has been taken all that is his, all that he has visioned in nature, all that has come to him from infinite sources, he then, truly, will be a dead Indian.

In Indian tradition, the Indian himself is the off-spring of Mother Earth and Father Sky. Accordingly, the poetry of Indians, their chants and rituals, their legends and their art all speak of nature's harmonies. In the following songs and poems, the Indian shows his fascination with — and reverence for — the natural world and all its creatures.

THE SONG OF THE STARS
(*Algonquin*)

We are the stars which sing,
We sing with our light;
We are the birds of fire,
We fly over the sky.
Our light is a voice;
We make a road for spirits,
For the spirits to pass over.
Among us are three hunters
Who chase a bear;
There never was a time
When they were not hunting.
We look down on the mountains.
This is the Song of the Stars.

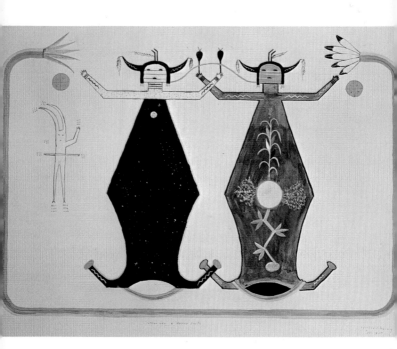

FATHER SKY AND MOTHER EARTH, *Navaho*
Edmund Tracy (Owi Po), Watercolor on paper

SONG OF THE SKY LOOM (*Tewa*)

O our Mother the Earth, O our Father the Sky,
Your children are we, and with tired backs
We bring you the gifts that you love.
Then weave for us a garment of brightness,
May the warp be the white light of morning,
May the weft be the red light of evening,
May the fringes be the falling rain,
May the border be the standing rainbow.
Thus weave for us a garment of brightness
That we may walk fittingly where birds sing,
That we may walk fittingly where grass is green
O our Mother the Earth, O our Father the Sky!

THE CREATION OF MAN (*Navajo*)

The gods and the spirits of the Sacred Mountains created Man. He was made of all rains, springs, rivers, ponds, black clouds, and sky. His feet are made of earth and his legs of lightning. White shell forms his knees, and his body is white and yellow corn; his flesh is of daybreak, his hair darkness; his eyes are of the sun. White corn forms his teeth, black corn his eyebrows, and red coral beads his nose. His tears are of rain, his tongue of straight lightning, and his voice of thunder. His heart is obsidian; the little whirlwind keeps his nerves in motion, and his movement is the air. The name of this new kind of being was "Created from Everything."

THE SOWER (*Navajo*)

I hold pollen of Dawn
In my hand,
With it I sow the night;
Over the mountain
Spring the first, pale blades
Of the new day.

SONG FOR THE NEWBORN (*Pueblo*)

Newborn, on the naked sand
Nakedly lay it.
Next to the earth mother,
That it may know her;
Having good thoughts of her, the food giver.

Newborn, we tenderly
In our arms take it,
Making good thoughts.
House-god, be entreated,
That it may grow from childhood to manhood,
Happy, contented;
Beautifully walking
The trail to old age.
Having good thoughts of the earth its mother,
That she may give it the fruits of her being.
Newborn, on the naked sand
Nakedly lay it.

INDIAN HORSES, *Jicarilla Apache*
Calvin Vigil, Watercolor on paper

This Yuma song depicts the mockingbird as a symbol
of happiness and the harmony of the universe:

SONG OF THE MOCKINGBIRD (*Yuma*)

"Thin little clouds are spread
Across the blue of the sky,
Thin little clouds are spread —
Oh, happy am I as I sing,
I sing of the clouds in the sky."

Thus tells the bird,
'Tis the mockingbird who sings,
And I stop to hear,
For he is glad at heart
And I will list to his message.

Then up the hill,
Up the hill I go my straight road,
The road of good —
Up the hill I go my straight road,
The happy road and good.

In Navajo legend, it is the bright, happy bluebird
that summons the sun to the sky each morning:

DAYBREAK SONG (*Navajo*)

All night the gods were with us,
Now night is gone;
Silence the rattle,
Sing the daybreak song,
For in the dawn Bluebird calls,
With voice melodious, Bluebird calls,
And out from his blankets of tumbled gray
The Sun comes, combing his hair for the day.

THE LIGHTS (*Navajo*)

The Sun is a luminous shield
Borne up the blue path
By a god;
The Moon is the torch
Of an old man
Who stumbles over stars.

THE PLANTING SONG (*Osage*)

I have made a footprint, a sacred one.
I have made a footprint; through it
  the blades push upward.
I have made a footprint; through it the blades
  radiate.
I have made a footprint; over it the blades
  float in the wind.
I have made a footprint; over it the ears lean
  toward one another.
I have made a footprint; over it I pluck the ears.
I have made a footprint; over it I bend
  the stalk to pluck the ears.
I have made a footprint; over it the blossoms
  lie gray.
I have made a footprint; smoke arises from my
  house.
I have made a footprint; there is cheer in my
  house.
I have made a footprint; I live in the light of day.

WAAYATA (SIOUX SEER), *Sioux*

Oscar Howe, 1952, Casein tempera on paper

Henry Wadsworth Longfellow derived much material for his Song of Hiawatha *from Henry Rowe Schoolcraft's studies of the myths and legends of the Ojibway Indians. The following story, adapted from Schoolcraft's researches, is an Indian allegory of Winter and Spring:*

PEBOAN AND SEEGWUM

Long ago an old man sat alone in his lodge beside a frozen stream. The fire was dying out, and it was near the end of winter. Outside the lodge, the cold wind swept before it the drifting snow. So the old man sat alone, day after day, until at last a young warrior entered his lodge. He was fresh and joyous and youthful.

The old man welcomed him. He drew out his long pipe and filled it with tobacco. He lighted it from the dying embers of the fire. Then they smoked together.

The old man said, "I blow my breath and the streams stand still. The water becomes stiff and hard like the stones."

"I breathe," said the warrior, "and flowers spring up over the plain."

"I shake my locks," said the old man, "and snow covers the land. Leaves fall from the trees. The birds fly away. The animals hide. The earth becomes hard."

"I shake my locks," said the young man, "and the warm rain falls. Plants blossom; the birds return; the streams flow."

Then the sun came up over the edge of the Earth-plain, and began to climb the trail through the Sky-land. The old man slept. Behold! The frozen stream nearby began to flow. The fire in the lodge died out. Robins sat upon the lodge poles and sang.

Then the warrior looked upon the sleeping old man. Behold! It was Peboan, the Winter-maker.

WIND SONG (*Pima*)

Far on the desert ridges
Stands the cactus;
Lo, the blossoms swaying
To and fro, the blossoms swaying, swaying.

As in Navajo legend the bluebird summons the sun,
so in Zuñi legend the swallow beckons the rain:

CORN-GRINDING SONG (*Zuñi*)

Yonder, yonder see the fair rainbow,
See the rainbow brightly decked and painted!
Now the swallow bringeth glad news to your corn,
Singing, "Hitherward, hitherward, hitherward, rain,
    Hither come!"
Singing, "Hitherward, hitherward, hitherward,
  white cloud,
    Hither come!"
Now we hear the corn-plants murmur,
    "We are growing everywhere!"
    Hi, yai, the world, how fair!

HARVEST DANCE, *San Ildefonso*

Awa Tsireh, 1920s, Watercolor on paper

HARVEST SONG (*Navajo*)

Corn is ripe,
The corn is ready to be gathered,
In piles we sort the colored corn.
Blue corn, white corn, yellow corn, red corn —
Food for the People.
Blue corn ground fine on the rubbing stone,
Blue corn for the ceremonies,
Blue corn for the thin bread
That cooks on the hot rock,
Blue corn, the sweetest,
For the thin bread rolled up into a stick.
Red corn rubbed fine on the stone,
Red corn made square,
Red corn wrapped in husks,
Red corn baked in the ashes.
White corn baked in the ashes.
Bread for the People,
Food for the People.
So all is well,
So all is well,
So all is well.

Many songs of the American Indian are songs of the heart — of love and devotion, of happiness and sorrow, of loneliness and despair. In the songs that follow, one can perceive the depth of the Indian's feeling for his loved ones:

PAPAGO LOVE SONGS

I
Early I rose
In the blue morning;
My love was up before me,
It came running to me from the doorways of
    the Dawn.

On Papago Mountain
The dying quarry
Looked at me with my love's eyes.

II
Do you long, my Maiden,
For bisnaga blossoms
To fasten in your hair?

I will pick them for you.
What are bisnaga spines to me
Whom love is forever pricking in the side?

NEITHER SPIRIT NOR BIRD (*Shoshone*)

Neither spirit nor bird;
That was my flute you heard
Last night by the river.
When you came with your wicker jar
Where the river drags the willows,
That was my flute you heard,
Wacoba, Wacoba,
Calling, Come to the willows!

Neither the wind nor a bird
Rustled the lupine blooms.
That was my blood you heard
Answer your garment's hem
Whispering through the grasses;
That was my blood you heard
By the wild rose under the willows.

That was no beast that stirred,
That was my heart you heard,
Pacing to and fro
In the ambush of my desire,
To the music my flute let fall.
Wacoba, Wacoba,
That was my heart you heard
Leaping under the willows.

ALGONQUIN LOVE SONG

O! come my beloved and climb with me,
That shining mountainside —
We'll watch the beautiful sun go down,
And talk of the leaves so sere and brown;
And the day you will be my bride,
We'll sit till the beautiful traveller of night
Shines high, o'er the mountainside.

We'll watch the little stars follow their chief,
And the Northern Lights play ball;
The Lightning winking, and lighting her pipe,
We'll list to the Thunder Bird beat with his
    might,
And the Whirlwind race with the Squall.
We will sit till all living creatures sleep;
But we'll not go to sleep at all.

We will sit on the beautiful mountain, nor mind,
The owl's shrill "Go to sleep all!"
We will watch the stars in their sleepless flight,
As they travel above us the whole of the night,
For they do not mind it at all.
We will sit more closely together, and think,
Of ourselves, and that is all.

TULE LOVE SONG (*Yaqui*)

Many pretty flowers, red, blue, and yellow.
We say to the girls, "Let us go and walk among
    the flowers."
The wind comes and sways the flowers.
The girls are like that when they dance.
Some are wide-open, large flowers and some are tiny
    little flowers.
The birds love the sunshine and the starlight,
The flowers smell sweet
The girls are sweeter than the flowers.

THE YIELDING HEART (*Yokut*)

Too soon I yield, I fear,
Too soon!
Yet yielding I rejoice
That in your touch
Such power should be,
Such magic in your voice!

LOVE CHARM

All during the night I dream of him.
And as soon as it is daylight
I get up and dress
And slip out and wait for him
To see if perhaps he will come by.

And when at last I see him coming toward me
My heart pounds
And I am afraid to look at him.
I do not raise my eyes.
He passes close by me
And sometimes he gives me a flower
He has picked
Or a sweet grass he has twisted
Into a bracelet.
And I wear the flower
Even when it is wilted.
And I wear the bracelet
Until it falls to pieces.

But when he is gone again
I raise my eyes
And look at him.
And I say this charm while I look at him
So that he must come back to me.
I say:
Suwa!
May you turn back
And look at me!

May you see only me
Wherever you look!

May you think about me
All through the day and the night!

May you come here to me every day!
May you love me as I love you!

I say this and I cry to myself. I cry and cry.

HER FIRST DANCE, *Santa Clara*
Pablita Velarde, 1954, Watercolor on paper

MAIDEN'S SONG (*Navajo*)

In the dawn, the Running in the dawn,
She wears long loops of turquoise in her ears,
Long loops of the sky-blue beads.
Around her neck beads of white shell.
On her arms bracelets of silver,
Bracelets with turquoise.
On her fingers rings of silver with turquoise.
On her feet moccasins of red buckskin
With silver buttons.
Her dress is velvet above, and blue;
Her dress is full below, and brown.
She sewed her dress in her mother's hogan.
She made ready for the Running at dawn.
She washed her hair; she brushed her hair
And tied it with white yarn.
She has learned to make fine blankets.
Good blankets, like her mother.
She owns many sheep and goats.
A brave man comes from the People.
There is a marriage ceremony
And he takes her to a new hogan,
With her sheep and her goats,
With her blanket sticks,
With her silver and sky-colored stones.
In the new hogan there is beauty,
There is beauty,
There is beauty.

SONGS OF OJIBWAY LOVERS

The Brave to the Maiden

Awake! flower of the forest, sky-treading bird of the prairie. Awake! awake! wonderful fawn-eyed One. When you look upon me I am satisfied, as flowers that drink dew. The breath of your mouth is the fragrance of flowers in the morning, your breath is their fragrance at evening in the moon-of-fading-leaf. Do not the red streams of my veins run toward you as forest-streams to the sun in the moon of bright nights?

When you are beside me my heart sings; a branch it is, dancing, dancing before the Wind-spirit in the moon of strawberries. When you frown upon me, beloved, my heart grows dark — a shining river the shadows of clouds darken, then with your smiles comes the sun and makes to look like gold furrows the cold wind drew in the water's face. Myself! behold me! blood of my beating heart. Earth smiles — the waters smile — even the sky-of-clouds smiles — but I, I lose the way of smiling when you are not near.

Awake! awake! my beloved.

The Maiden to the Brave

My love is tall and graceful as the young pine waving on the hill, and as swift in his course as the noble, stately deer; his hair is flowing, and dark as the blackbird that floats through the air, and his eyes, like the eagle's, both piercing and bright; his heart, it is fearless and great, and his arm it is strong in the fight, as this bow made of ironwood which he easily bends. His aim is as sure in the fight and chase, as the hawk, which ne'er misses its prey. Ah, aid me, ye spirits! of water, of earth, and of sky, while I sing in his praise, and my voice shall be heard, it shall ring through the sky, and echo, repeating the same, shall cause it to swell in the breadth of the wind; and his fame shall be spread throughout the land, and his name shall be known beyond the lakes.

BUFFALO AND DEER DANCE, *Cochiti*
Quah Ah, ca. 1930s, Watercolor on paper

Of all the American Indian's tribal events, none was as important to him as War and The Hunt. Both were enacted in the shadow of danger — thus both were expressions of manhood. Both were surrounded by elaborate ritual and ceremony. And both, as we see on the following pages, are celebrated in chant, poem and song:

A SONG OF THE DEER CEREMONY
(*San Carlos Apache*)

At the east,
Where the jet ridges of the earth lie. . . .

At the south,
Where the white shell ridges of the earth lie,
Where all kinds of fruit are ripe,
We two will meet.

From there where the coral ridges of the earth lie,
We two will meet.
Where the ripe fruits are fragrant,
We two will meet.

HUNTING-SONG (*Navajo*)

Comes the deer to my singing,
Comes the deer to my song,
Comes the deer to my singing.

He, the blackbird, he am I,
Bird beloved of the wild deer.
    Comes the deer to my singing.

From the Mountain Black,
From the summit,
Down the trail, coming, coming now,
    Comes the deer to my singing.

Through the blossoms,
Through the flowers, coming, coming now,
    Comes the deer to my singing.

Through the flower dew-drops,
    Coming, coming now,
    Comes the deer to my singing.

Through the pollen, flower pollen,
    Coming, coming now,
    Comes the deer to my singing.

Starting with his left fore-foot,
Stamping, turns the frightened deer.
  Comes the deer to my singing.

Quarry mine, blessed am I
In the luck of the chase.
  Comes the deer to my singing.

  Comes the deer to my singing,
  Comes the deer to my song,
  Comes the deer to my singing.

Most Indian tribes had special chants that prepared them for mortal combat. Following is one of the first such war songs to be translated into English:

HEAR MY VOICE

Hear my voice, Birds of War!
I prepare a feast for you to feed on;
I see you cross the enemy's lines;
Like you I shall go.
I wish the swiftness of your wings;
I wish the vengeance of your claws;
I muster my friends;
I follow your flight.
Ho, you young men warriors,
Bear your angers to the place of fighting!

SIOUX EAGLE DANCER, *Sioux*

Oscar Howe, 1954, Casein tempera on paper

LAMENT OF A MAN FOR HIS SON

Son, my son!

I will go up to the mountain
And there I will light a fire
To the feet of my son's spirit,
And there will I lament him;
Saying,
O my son,
What is my life to me, now you are departed!

Son, my son,
In the deep earth
We softly laid thee in a Chief's robe,
In a warrior's gear.
Surely there,
In the spirit land
Thy deeds attend thee!
Surely,
The corn comes to the ear again!

But I, here,
I am the stalk that the seed-gatherers
Descrying empty, afar, left standing.
Son, my son!
What is my life to me, now you are departed?

WARRIOR'S SONG

Weep not for me, Loved Woman,
Should I die:
But for yourself be weeping!

Weep not for warriors who go
Gladly to battle.
Theirs to revenge
Fallen and slain of our people;
Theirs to lay low
All our foes like them,
Death to make, singing.

Weep not for warriors,
But weep for women!
Oh, weep for all women!

Theirs to be pitied
Most of all creatures,
Whose men return not!
How shall their hearts be stayed
When we are fallen?

Weep not for me, Loved Woman,
For yourself alone be weeping!

Wah-pah-nah-yah
(Dick West)

Religion has always played a large role in the In-dian's life. To the American Indian, the purpose of religion is to bring happiness into the world. Creator of the world is the "Great Spirit" — known by one tribe as Manito, *by another as* Wakan-Tanka, *and by still another as* Tirawa. *The Great Spirit rules the universe, smiling in sunshine and showers, frowning in whirlwinds and storms. Much Indian literature attempts to define the relationship between the In-dian and his God:*

GIFTS OF THE GODS (*Navajo*)

They have given me of soft goods,
Good and beautiful skins and furs,
And of hard goods, beads and haliotis shells,
Of many domestic animals
And of animals to hunt,
Corn of the rainbow color,
Black clouds, mists, male-rains,
Lightning, plants, and pollen
For my voice, my limbs, my mind;
I am beautiful
In gratitude.

MEDICINE BUNDLE OPENING, *Cheyenne*
Dick West, early 1950s, Watercolor on paper   41

PRAYER (*Zuñi*)

My fathers,
Our sun father,
Our mothers,
Dawn
As you arise and come out to your sacred place,
I pass you on your road.
The source of our flesh,
White corn,
Prayer meal,
Shell,
Pollen,
I offer to you.
Our sun father,
To you I offer prayer meal,
To you we offer it.
To you we offer pollen.
According to the words of my prayer
Even so may it be.
There shall be no deviation.
Sincerely
From my heart I send forth my prayers.
To you prayer meal.
Shell I offer,
Pollen I offer,
According to the words of my prayer.

A NAVAJO PRAYER

At Sky-Reaching-Butte,
At House-Made-of-Darkness,
Black pollen with which he conceals his body,
Black-Horned-Rattler, young chief, your sacrifice
   I have made,
Your smoke I have prepared.
This day I have become your child,
This day your grandchild I have become.

Watch over me.
Hold your hand before me in protection.
Stand before me and arise as my protector.
Do my commands as I do your bidding.
Let no harm befall me from the air as I breathe,
From the rain as it falls, from the Thunders as
   they strike,
From below the plants, from the trees under which
   water flows.
Dewdrops and pollen may I enjoy.
With these may it be beautiful before me.
With these may it be beautiful behind me.
All is beautiful again, all is restored in beauty.

NAVAHO PATIENT, *Navaho*

Beatien Yazz, 1950s, Casein tempera on paper

Traditionally, a shaman, *or "medicine man," is one who possesses the secret of communion with the gods. Here is the chant of a Navajo shaman as he fights for the life of a sick warrior:*

MEDICINES

I go in the early morning
Before the sun is up
To gather fever medicine,
White frost from a yucca cup.

I catch the blue bird singing
The last notes of his song
And pop him into your pollen
To make you strong.

I gather the four sweet waters
Of hail and river and snow
Mixed with the drop of the spring rock;
Clean from them you go.

And in the lightning flashes
I pluck blue ears of corn;
With sacred gruel I shall feed you
That you may be reborn.

In the following story, a Sioux chief explains the significance of "The Sacred Pipe" — a symbol for life itself — and tells how it came to his people.

THE LEGEND OF THE SACRED PIPE

Early one morning, very many winters ago, two Lakota were out hunting with their bows and arrows, and as they were standing on a hill looking for game, they saw in the distance something coming toward them in a very strange and wonderful manner. When this mysterious thing came nearer to them, they saw that it was a very beautiful woman, dressed in white buckskin, and bearing a bundle on her back. . . .

She took from her back the bundle, and holding it with both hands in front of the chief, said: "Behold this and always love it! It is *lela wakan* [very sacred], and you must treat it as such. No impure man should ever be allowed to see it, for within this bundle there is a sacred pipe. With this you will, during the winters to come, send your voices to *Wakan-Tanka*, your Father and Grandfather."

After the mysterious woman said this, she took from the bundle a pipe, and also a small round stone which she placed upon the ground. Holding the pipe up with its stem to the heavens, she said: "With this sacred pipe you will walk upon the Earth; for the

46

Earth is your Grandmother and Mother, and She is sacred. Every step that is taken upon Her should be as a prayer. The bowl of this pipe is of red stone; it is the Earth. Carved in the stone and facing the center is this buffalo calf who represents all the four-leggeds who live upon your Mother. The stem of the pipe is of wood, and this represents all that grows upon the Earth. And these twelve feathers which hang here where the stem fits into the bowl are from *Wambli Galeshka*, the Spotted Eagle [spirit of the Intellect], and they represent the eagle and all the wingeds of the air. All these peoples, and all the things of the universe, are joined to you who smoke the pipe — all send their voices to *Wakan-Tanka*, the Great Spirit.

Moving around the lodge in a sun-wise manner, the mysterious woman left, but after walking a short distance she looked back towards the people and sat down. When she rose the people were amazed to see that she had become a young red and brown buffalo calf. Then this calf walked farther, lay down, and rolled, looking back at the people, and when she got up she was a white buffalo. Again the white buffalo walked farther and rolled on the ground, becoming now a black buffalo. This buffalo then walked farther away from the people, stopped, and after bowing to each of the four quarters of the universe, disappeared over the hill.

SHALAKO AND MUDHEADS, *San Ildefonso*
Awa Tsireh, 1920s, Watercolor on paper

BENEDICTORY CHANT (*Navajo*)

Now Talking God,
With your feet I walk,
I walk with your limbs,
I carry forth your body,
For me your mind thinks,
Your voice speaks for me.
Beauty is before me
And beauty behind me,
Above and below me hovers the beautiful,
I am surrounded by it,
I am immersed in it.
In my youth I am aware of it,
And in old age
I shall walk quietly
The beautiful trail.

The freedom of native Americans was seriously ham-
pered by the encroachments of modern civilization.
Having known nothing but natural barriers to his
movements about the continent, the Indian has had
some difficulty adjusting to the new order. Here are
expressions of modern Indians as they see the sun set
on the days of their grandparents:

THE NEW DIRECTION
by Emerson Blackhorse Mitchell

This vanishing old road,
    Through hail-like dust storm,
It stings and scratches,
    Stuffy, I cannot breathe.

Here once walked my ancestors,
    I was told by the old ones,
One can dig at the very spot,
    And find forgotten implements.

Wasting no time I urged on,
    Where I'd stop I knew not,
Startled I listened to the wind,
    It whistled, screamed, cried,
"You! Go back, not this path!"

Then I recalled this trail
    Swept away by the north wind,
It wasn't for me to follow,
    The trail of the Long Walk.

Deciding between two cultures,
    I gave a second thought,
Reluctantly I took the new one,
    The paved rainbow highway.
I had found a new direction.

THE FOLDING FAN *by Grey Cohoe*

The wild beauty of an eagle, once born to virgin sky
   now held in a sacred fan.
                        Beaded feathers
stiffen the grasp, the fingers that curled
to ease the cold soul but let the agony tear,
   for the heart will weep all the same.
Never again is life made vivid
   or for who else the kind warmth?
Maybe this I know, that it is for the dying,
whose ending breaths I hear not, as the wisdom
                       will come no more,
   only to grave, olden with age.
Eternity flies now on the wings of the gone soul,
                     never to be seen.

   Listen,
a drum I hear, distance, yet;
       it's from the folding fan.
           The preying bird of death is waiting,
           calling.

PEYOTE SINGERS, *Hopi*

Quayavema, ca. 1940s, Casein tempera on paper   53

RED EAGLE *by Janet Campbell*

Red Eagle,
Cold, dead, noble, Red Eagle.
Tomorrow they will bury you in Black Hill.
They think you have left me forever.
When I grow lonely for you
    I will walk into the night
    and listen to your brother, the wind.
He will tell me if you want me.
I will follow the path through the forest
    upon which your moccasins
    have trod so many times.
I will hear the night sounds
    you have told me about.
I will walk into the valley of Minnelosa,
    the sweet grass.
In the white moonlight I will pray.
I will pray to the spirits
    and they will speak to me
    as they have spoken to you before.
Then I will touch your tree
    and you will softly whisper to me.
    You will whisper to me,
    Red Eagle, Red Eagle,
    Upon the mountain.

INDIAN LOVE LETTER *by Soge Track*

Lady of the crescent moon
tonight I look at the sky
You are not there
You are not mad at me, are you?
"You are angry at the people,
Yes. I know."
   they are changing
   be not too hard
If you were taken
   to the mission school,
not because you wanted,
but someone thought it best for you
you too would change.

They came out of nowhere
telling us how to eat our food
how to build our homes
how to plant our crops.
Need I say more of what they did?
All is new — the old ways are nothing.
   they are changing
   be not too hard

CHOCTAW BALL DANCERS, *Choctaw*
Terry Saul, 1951, Watercolor on paper

I talk to them
they turn their heads.
Do not be hurt — you have me
I live by the old ways
I will not change.

Tonight — my prayer plumes in hand
with the white shell things —
to the silent place I will go
(It is for you I go, please be there.)
Oh! Lady of the crescent moon
with the corn-silk hair — I love you
    they are changing
    be not too hard

I AM CRYING FROM THIRST
by Alonzo Lopez

I am crying from thirst.
I am singing for rain.
I am dancing for rain.
The sky begins to weep,
    for it sees me
    singing and dancing
    on the dry, cracked
    earth.

PERSIMMON WINE *by Winston Weathers*
A Chorale for Lonely People in the Osage Hills

Persimmons fall. And we shall make
    persimmon wine. (We shall come
    with jars of music into the corners of
    our sorrow.)

And winter shall pass. I have seen it fade
    along the forsaken creeks of the
    Osage, between Okesa and Nelagony,
    Gray Horse and Pswhuska. I have seen
    it fade through Burbank, Fairfax,
    Wizzbang, and Hominy. (Those are the names
    of Indian towns.)

Do not be afraid. We shall drink
    persimmon wine! Come when the hills
    begin to shake with their green and
    silent passion. Come when the hills
    catch fire with April and the smoke of
    the redbud tree lies across the prairie.
    Come when the water's green, and
    venturing, and first alive.

Pour from the crocks the miracle of wine.
Who is afraid of what we might have
been? Or what, so long ago, we
chanced to be? (But do not die before
the wine is done. Live for the wine
that we have made. Live for the
drinking of the wine that is to come.)

Persimmon wine. And dancing upon the
waters: Bird Creek and Sand Creek
and the Caney River. And through the
sweeping valleys of the sumac and
the sandstone.

Persimmon wine. And dancing upon the
face of time: Longhorn cattle far from
home, the Brahman bulls, the push
and pull of oil beneath the ground,
the Katy railcars weeping on the
wooden trestles, nameless outlaws
starving in the shadows of the caves.
Dancing! Like the driven horses,
scattering and laughing in the fields of
Bigheart, in the pasturelands of Hulah
and Wynona. (Those are the names of
Indian towns.)

We shall make persimmon wine. And
  drink the wine. And then lie down.
  We shall strip to the wet and loving
  roots. Oaks. And cottonwood.
  And sassafras. And sycamore. (The
  sky is blue with thunder.) Should we
  not lie together, the music on our lips?

Sundown over Little Chief. Sweet is the
  sound of silence. There is a sudden
  flight of mourning doves. The
  sun-lashed rain is catching in our hair.
  (We shall make persimmon wine.
  You come!)

And when the future finds us, let them
  say, "They were a magic people in
  this ordinary place."

PICTOGRAPH ALTAR, *Cochiti*

Joe Herrera, 1952, Casein tempera on paper   61

Set in Intertype Walbaum, a light, open typeface
designed by Justus Erich Walbaum (1768-1839),
who was a typefounder at Weimar.
Printed on Crown Royale Book paper.
Pictures courtesy of the Denver Art Museum.
The publisher gratefully acknowledges the cooperation
of Mr. Richard Conn, Curator of Native Arts,
in helping select these pictures.